Tombout or Tomboucto u
Niger Senegal R.
Country of
Meczara
Mura
the great Lake
forded over in
a dry season
K.M OF
Reghebil
ZEGZEG
les of Cafsan
oved of
opes and
or the
ry of
KINGDOM
OF GAGO
From whence
they carry
Gold to Moroko
Timby or
Lamby
Semegila
OF GUBER
the 2 City
of Ghana
Niger R.
KINGDOM
K.M OF
DAHOME
Kingdom
Sandy Plain
Guber
OF BIT o
Whose Inhabi
tants are very
Rich
TEMIAN
These People
are Antropopha
gos or Mencaters
Gago
Dau
ASIANTE
OR INTA
Akam
K. OF ULCUMA
OR ULCAMI
R. Volta
EA or Proper GUINEA
OLD COAST
Ardra
Nsem
ates of Usa
dependent
EGUIRA
ACAMBOUK
Sabyi
Soqua Ingo
James
Great
Acara
Apy
Ofr
Cape
R. Benin
Offra
Monte
Arambane
Boudedu
Forados
R. Pomba
C.º of Calbary
Kort Key
R. Volta
Chriftiansbourg
Fort Nassau
Cape forse de la Mina
I Forcados
Mocco Anadonis
Cape
3. Points
Tacorari
C Formosa
old Cathaw
I. of Amboies
Camerone
I. Fernand Po
Princes I
I Branca
S. Iohn
Corisco I.
Line
I. S.t Thomas
Povoasan
10 R. Gabo
The Meridian of London
A Scale of English Miles
45 90 180 270 360
C. Lopo
Gonsalves

To be placed faceing the Title

Series 117

This is a Ladybird Expert book, one of a series of titles for an adult readership. Written by some of the leading lights and outstanding communicators in their fields and published by one of the most trusted and well-loved names in books, the Ladybird Expert series provides clear, accessible and authoritative introductions, informed by expert opinion, to key subjects drawn from science, history and culture.

Dedicated to Joe

The Publisher would like to thank the following for the illustrative references for this book:
Endpapers: © The British Library Board; page 7: Granger, NYC/TopFoto;
page 43: Stirton/Reportage/Getty images.

Every effort has been made to ensure images are correctly attributed; however, if any omission or error has been made please notify the Publisher for correction in future editions.

MICHAEL JOSEPH

UK | USA | Canada | Ireland | Australia
India | New Zealand | South Africa

Michael Joseph is part of the Penguin Random House group of companies whose addresses can be found at global.penguinrandomhouse.com

Penguin Random House UK

First published 2018
001

Text copyright © Gus Caseley-Hayford

All images copyright © Ladybird Books Ltd, 2018

The moral right of the author has been asserted

Printed in Italy by L.E.G.O. S.p.A.

A CIP catalogue record for this book is available from the British Library
ISBN: 978-0-718-18910-5

www.greenpenguin.co.uk

MIX
Paper from responsible sources
FSC® C018179

Penguin Random House is committed to a sustainable future for our business, our readers and our planet. This book is made from Forest Stewardship Council® certified paper.

Timbuktu

Gus Casely-Hayford

with illustrations by
Angelo Rinaldi

Ladybird Books Ltd, London

City Beyond Reach

For centuries, it sat as a frustration: a jewel that lay defiantly beyond Europe's grasp. Unlike El Dorado, road-hardened merchants were confident that this conduit to the vast gold reserves of the Mali Empire existed.

Timbuktu was a prize that Europe coveted.

In 1618, a company was founded in London with the primary objective of building a trading relationship with Timbuktu. It would fail. As would generations of Europeans, their expeditions ending in murder, bungling, confusion – some simply disappearing without trace. The catalogue of calamity was long and tragic. In 1620, Englishman Richard Jobson mistook the River Gambia for the Niger; in 1670, Paul Imbert, a French sailor, was kidnapped and murdered en route; John Ledyard, an American, died in Cairo in 1789, before his expedition had even really begun; Daniel Houghton, an Irishman, simply vanished after leaving Gambia; and Frederick Horneman, a German academic, perished on the banks of the Niger. Even Mungo Park, one of the most celebrated explorers of any age, was to drown in the Niger under a hail of spears in 1806.

Timbuktu held its secrets dearly.

The first Westerner to return claiming to have seen Timbuktu, a shipwrecked African-American, Benjamin Rose, was kidnapped and taken to the city under duress in 1810. Rose was followed by Major Gordon Laing, who traversed the Sahara, reaching the city in 1826 only to be killed before he could return home. Laing was followed in 1828 by René Caillié, the first European to return alive, opening up the city on the edge of the Sahara to the West.

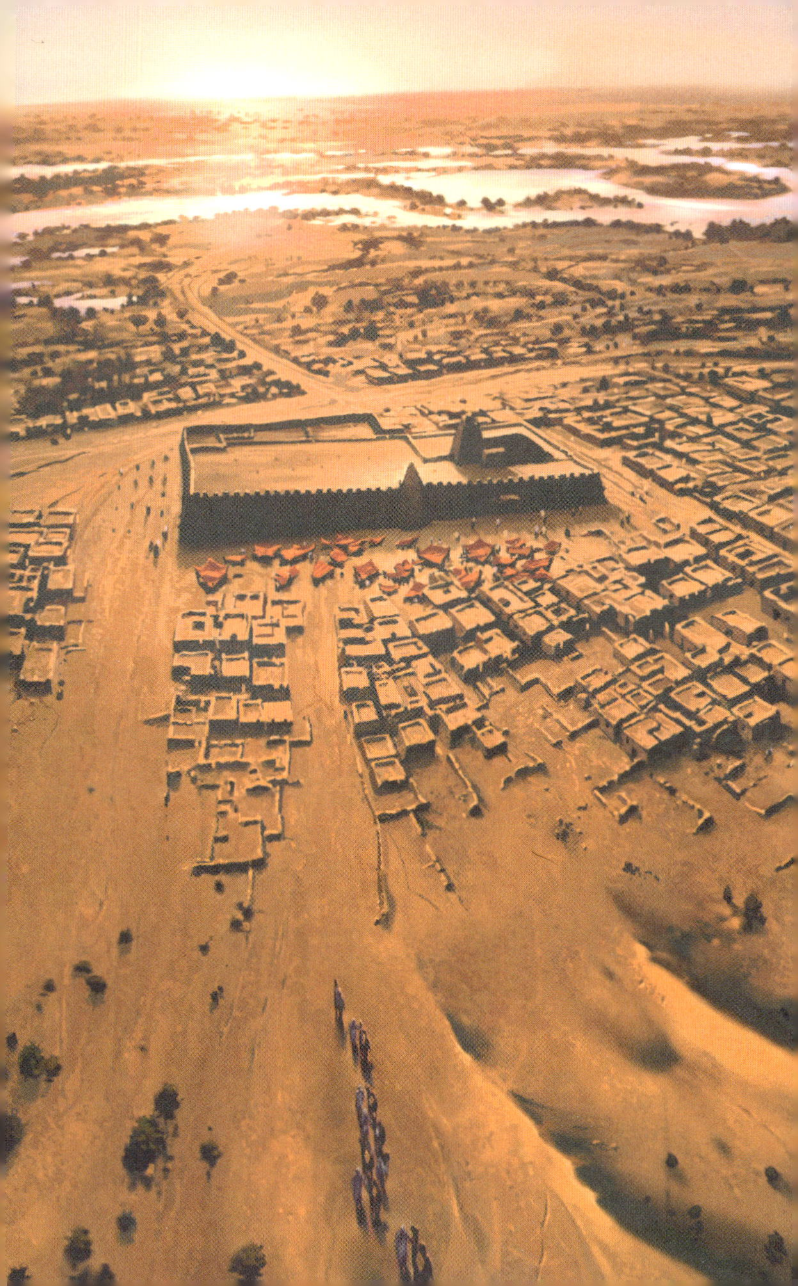

Geography

The River Niger is a remarkable piece of geography – flowing away from the sea, it draws its strength on the Guinea Highlands of West Africa, pulling clusters of streams into a single unanswerable body of water. It descends from a lush plateau, slowing as it winds northward through forested regions, across plains in defiance of formidable heat and topography. Languorously, it then pushes on towards the Sahara Desert, until at its most northerly point, it seasonally bursts into flower, disgorging vast amounts of water and silt across arid plains to form a life-giving delta in one of the most unforgiving landscapes on Earth: the Middle Niger, a green corridor of fertile land within which an empire could grow and thrive. And sitting on the ring finger of the River Niger's outstretched hand, was the jewel of the medieval world: Timbuktu.

Perfectly positioned on the desert frontier of the Mali Empire, Timbuktu grew to become a wealthy port for traders from across the Sahara, a gateway for West African goods that sought markets across North Africa and beyond. Yet, it was almost always more than just a place where sub-Saharan dealers in gold and copper could encounter traders conveying salt and spices southward. It also became the market for the exchange and development of ideas. It sat on the edge of a body of sand the size of the US, a desert that separated some of the most economically aggressive and culturally confident states of the medieval age. It was the perfect conduit between worlds, a place where Sudanic and Sahelo cultures, desert and tropic, came together to conceive something exceptional.

But this passage of history begins before the development of the Mali Empire and the transformation of Timbuktu.

A part of the Catalan Atlas, c. 1375.

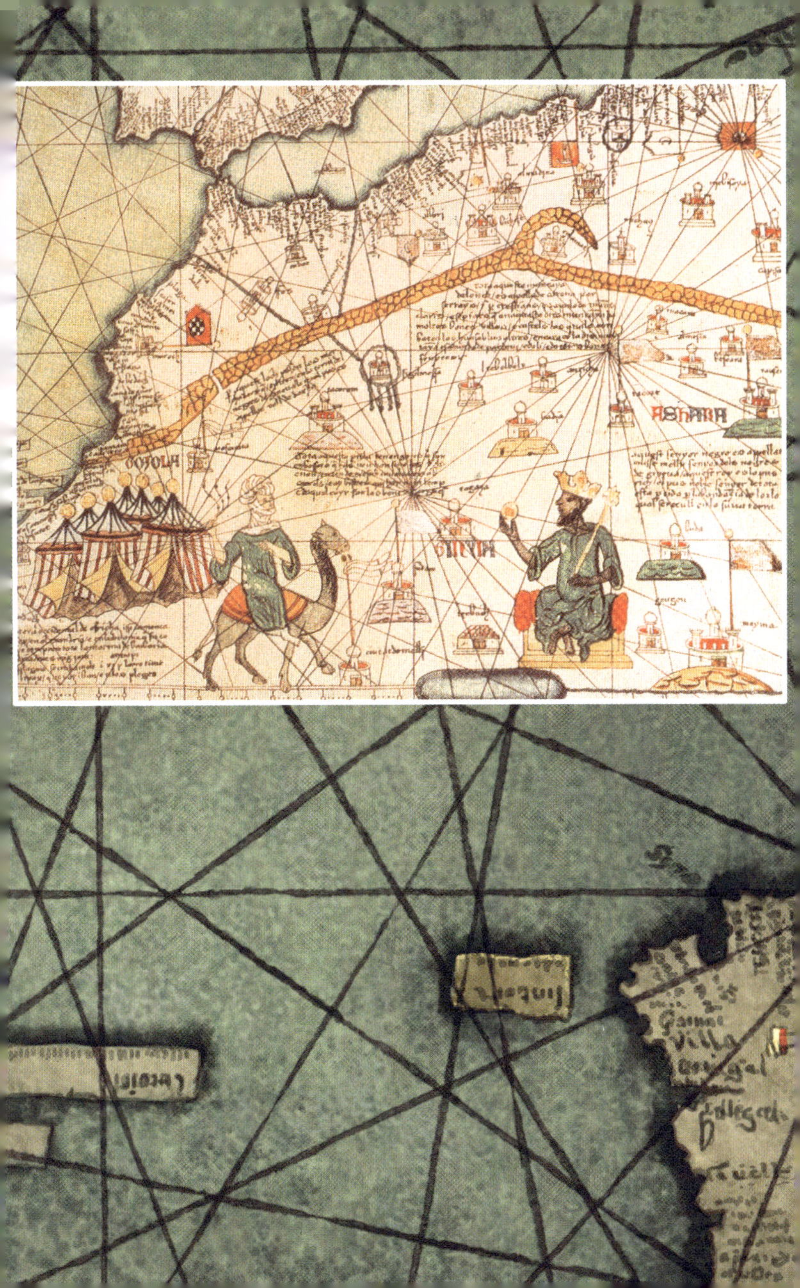

Rise and Fall of Ghana

With the rise of the great North African Berber Muslim dynasties from the seventh century came the opening up of ancient routes across and around the Sahara to a new generation of entrepreneurs. The introduction of the camel offered opportunities to exploit trans-Saharan trade at a level of intensity that was utterly transformational. The gold-rich region beneath the northern arm of the River Niger flourished. When Muhammad ibn Musa Al-Khwarizmi, the ninth-century Persian intellectual (who shaped thinking in mathematics, astronomy and trigonometry) rewrote Ptolemy's second-century *Geography*, he included amongst the new additions the Kingdom of Ghana.

In 1068, the Cordoban Muslim scholar Al-Bakri wrote, 'The King of Ghana, when he calls up his army, can put 200,000 men into the field, more than 40,000 of them archers.' The King levied tax on all imported salt and gold, allowing his subjects to sell gold-dust, but securing all gold nuggets for the crown. This was a powerful, well-governed state that practised a variety of forms of religion, but at court and in trade the ascendant religion was Islam, and the King seemed tolerant of this.

However, many of Ghana's neighbours were not comfortable with this cosmopolitan, liberal state growing rich on their efforts, particularly their ideologically conservative trading partners on the far side of the Sahara, the Berber Almoravids. When, in 1076, the Almoravids attacked, the armies and resources of the Ghana Kingdom were simply no match for their northern neighbours. With trade routes compromised and weakened by competition, and suffering unprecedented drought, the Ghana state began a long, slow demise.

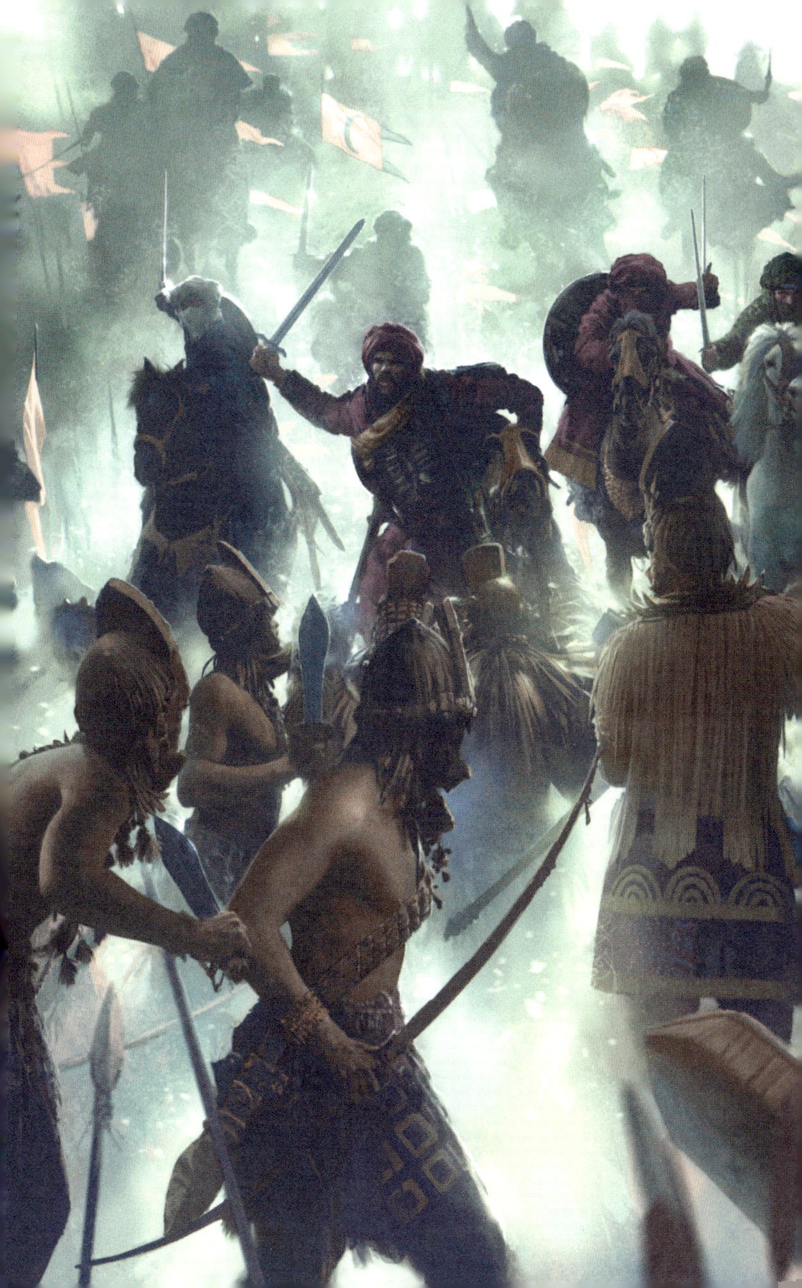

The Birth of Mali

The founder of the Mali Empire was Sunjata Keita. He was born in or at the turn of the thirteenth century, a time of profound flux. He would have grown up amongst the chaos of Ghana's demise, but perhaps learned something of the ancient cultures that had left their mark on the landscape in distant prehistory when the Sahara region was a fertile and thriving territory. He would have seen the transition between Berber dynasties in the north; he may have heard about the rise of the Ife to the south; and perhaps even the dominance of the Solomonic dynasty in Ethiopia to the east. It was a moment of African renaissance, of quickening change, and growing confidence across the continent as new, outwardly focused regimes began to build ambitious states as far afield as Great Zimbabwe and the Swahili Sultanates. Each one engaged directly or indirectly beyond the continent, and each was driven to invest in securing their intellectual and cultural legacy.

Sunjata Keita was ambitious too – and he wanted to build a modern state that would last.

It is believed that Sunjata was born in Niani on the banks of a tributary of the Niger – one of twelve brothers who belonged to the Keita royal family. One of his earliest, defining memories would have been when his home region, Kangaba, was attacked by the army of the formidable Blacksmith King, Sumaguru Kante, at the beginning of the thirteenth century. All Sunjata's brothers were killed and his sister, Nana Triban, was carried away to marry Sumaguru, leaving Sunjata the sole heir to the throne.

Destiny and revenge called – the name Sumaguru Kante would haunt Sunjata.

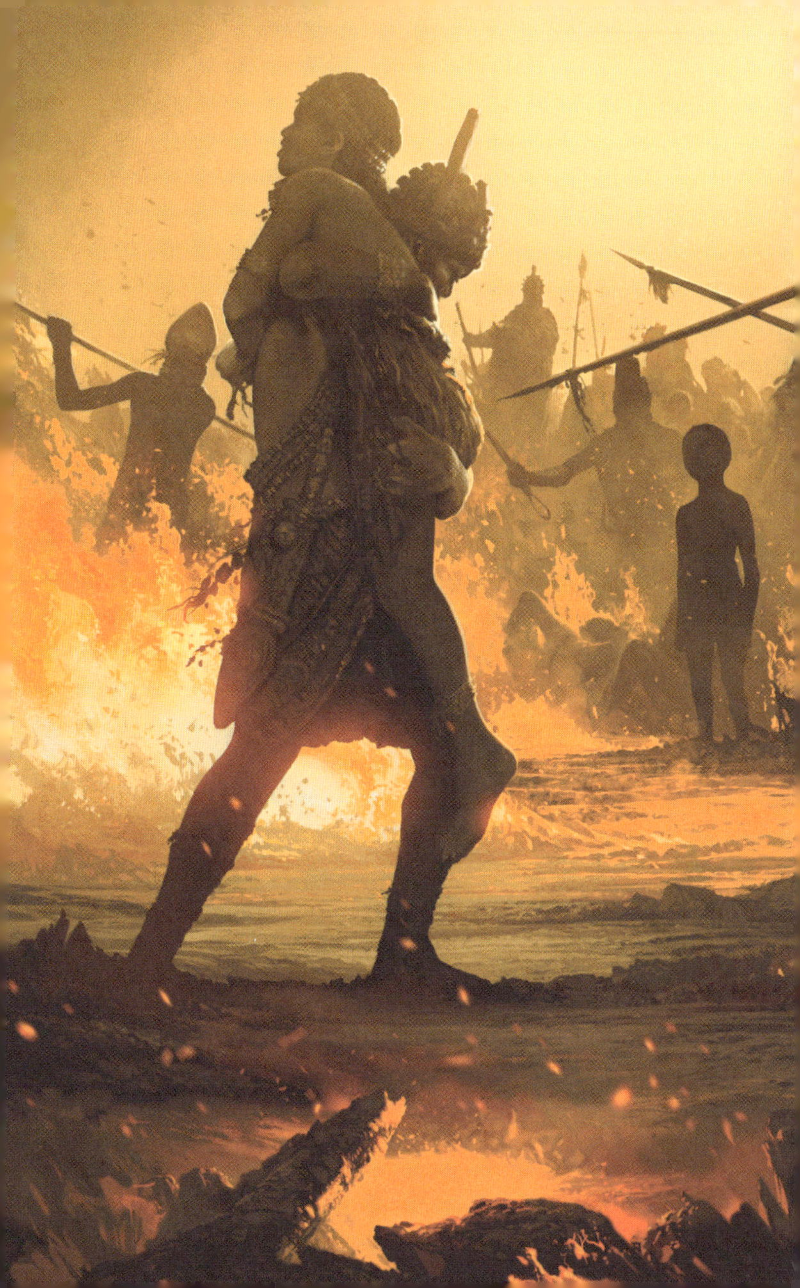

Sunjata

Like their Berber and Ethiopian contemporaries, the founders of the Mali Empire developed an epic saga of origin to bind people impregnably to the new empire. They made it as beautiful as the cave paintings of their antecedents, but they also learned from Muslim scholars who had visited the Ghana court, and they utilized griots – skilled orators, musicians and poets – to institutionalize and spread their story. It seemed to be part of a moment that reached beyond Africa, as around the globe, from the crusading Pope Innocent III to the ruthless Genghis Khan, narrative and military ambition developed hand in hand.

Sunjata's father was a Mandinka king, who was visited by a magical hunter, who prophesied that the King's son would become an epoch-defining monarch.

When, years later, Sogolon Conde, the Buffalo Woman, hobbled into his court, the King recognized that, despite her profound disabilities, this supernaturally gifted woman was destined to bear his special son. In the face of objections from his lawful wife, in defiance of the weight of convention and pressure from his court, Sogolon bore the King a son – Sunjata Keita.

Sunjata's early life was beset with challenges. He was ostracized at court and had inherited his mother's physical disabilities, which left him unable to walk. But the King saw beyond that. He recognized in his son both intellectual flair and charisma, and conferred upon Sunjata his own storyteller. And this wasn't any storyteller – this was the son of the court historian. In so doing, he symbolically passed on the legitimizing narrative that underpinned the state.

The story of Sunjata is still retold and sung to this day.

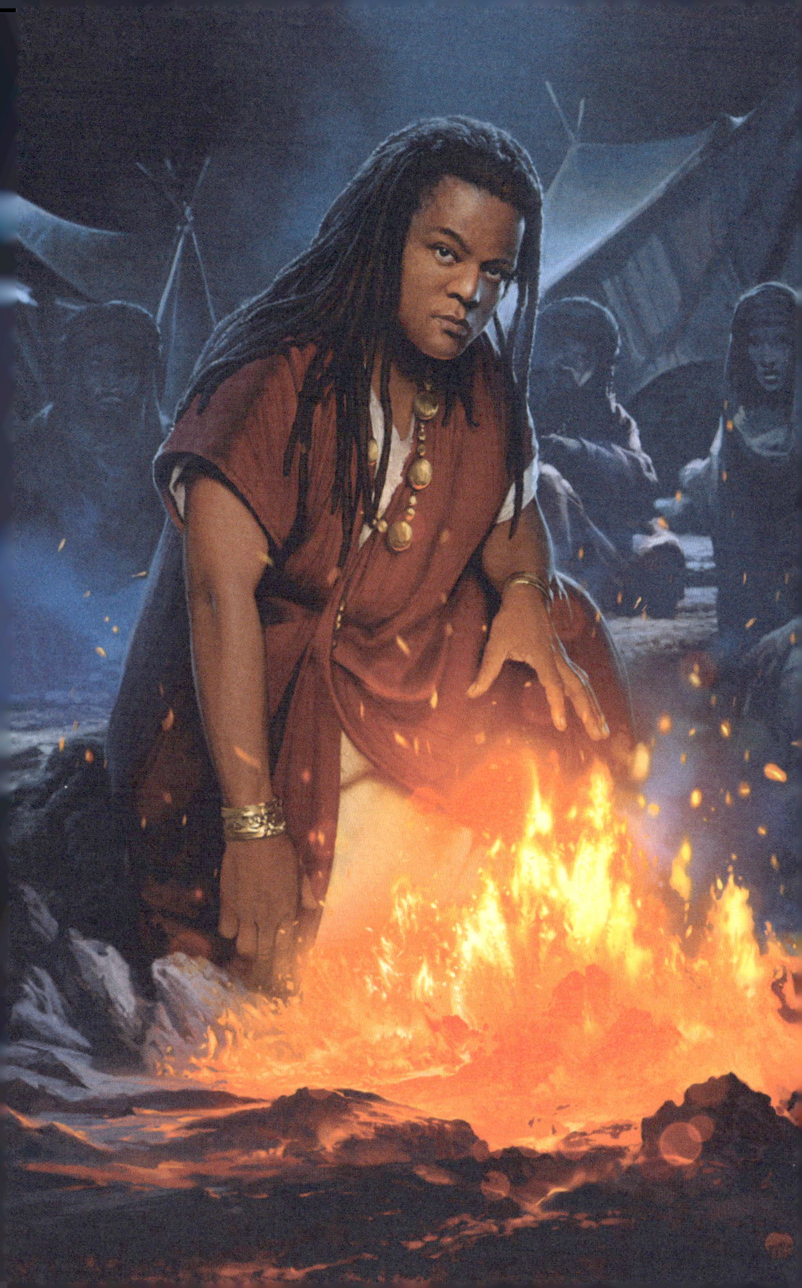

Exile

When his father died, Sunjata, the once favoured son, was forced to flee into exile, leaving the throne to his gloating elder brother.

Sunjata spent years fleeing as a refugee. It offered him experiences that would have been impossible at court, learning first-hand the realities of ordinary people's lives in the chaotic aftermath of the collapse of the Ghana state. He came to realize that not only was it his destiny to return to lead his people, but that in addressing his personal injustices, he might also be able to free his own people from the mismanagement of his half-brother.

Eventually Sunjata found refuge in the court of the benevolent King of Méma, Mansa Tunkara, where news reached him that his kingdom had been attacked by his family's old adversary, Sumaguru Kante, and the capital, had fallen. Sunjata knew that his time in the wilderness was at an end.

At the head of Mansa Tunkara's army, Sunjata began his campaign of Mandinka liberation, gathering together a complex alliance of peoples which represented the kind of cultural and religious diversity that had been the mark of old Ghana. Whilst that diversity had once led to fatal weakness and division, now, under new leadership and faced with a common threat, it was their strength.

At the Battle of Kirina, c.1235, buoyed by a sense of destiny and fuelled by a drive for revenge, Sunjata's forces overwhelmed Sumaguru Kante, and the Mali Empire was born. Sunjata was given the title *Mansa*, Emperor, and all the twelve regions that had answered his call to arms accepted him as their paramount leader.

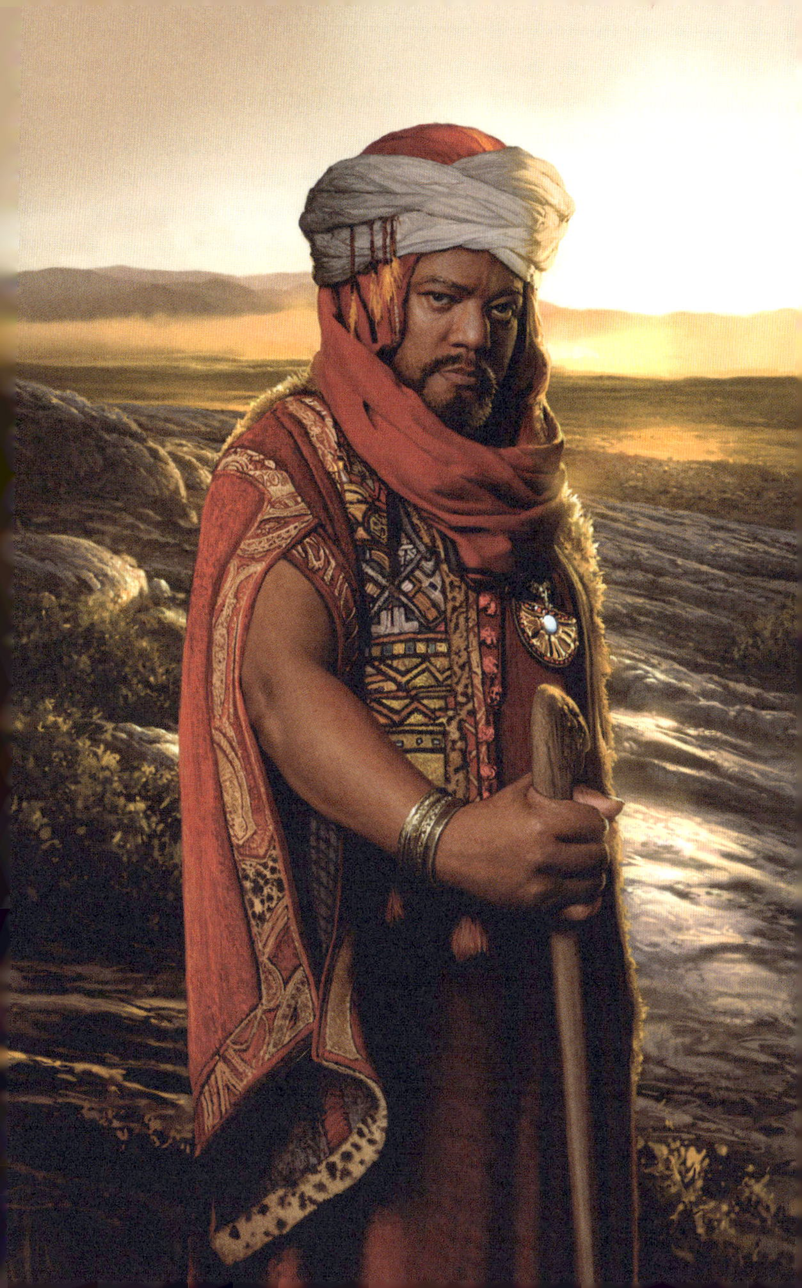

The Nurturing of Traditional Thinking

As the once mighty Sumaguru Kante fled the battlefield, he left behind a royal balofon – a ceremonial wooden xylophone – and a four-stringed kora, bequeathing the new Mali Empire beautiful sets of traditions that would come to define it culturally. Although this new empire would be united by Islam, it would also be founded upon traditional Mandinka institutions. When Ibn Battuta, the Berber traveller, visited the Mali Emperor Mansa Musa's court in 1325, a century later, he would remark on the beauty of its balofon traditions.

This was not just a tradition centred on art; it was a mechanism for formalizing record, for controlling historical narrative.

In defeating Sumaguru Kante, Sunjata had learned that societies might win wars if they were driven by a common goal. Similarly, Mali's founding fathers knew that peace would be won by embracing common cultural anchors. They would need mechanisms of common cultural expression to drive cohesion, and to demonstrate the power and beneficence of the monarchy and underpin law and governance. The court of the Mali Empire adopted pottery, fabric and other state crafts to draw people into their family, to engender a sense of identity, belonging and pride. But at the empire's core was narrative – institutionalized stories and narrative music – and, as Sunjata's father seemed to intuit, a storyteller: the griot.

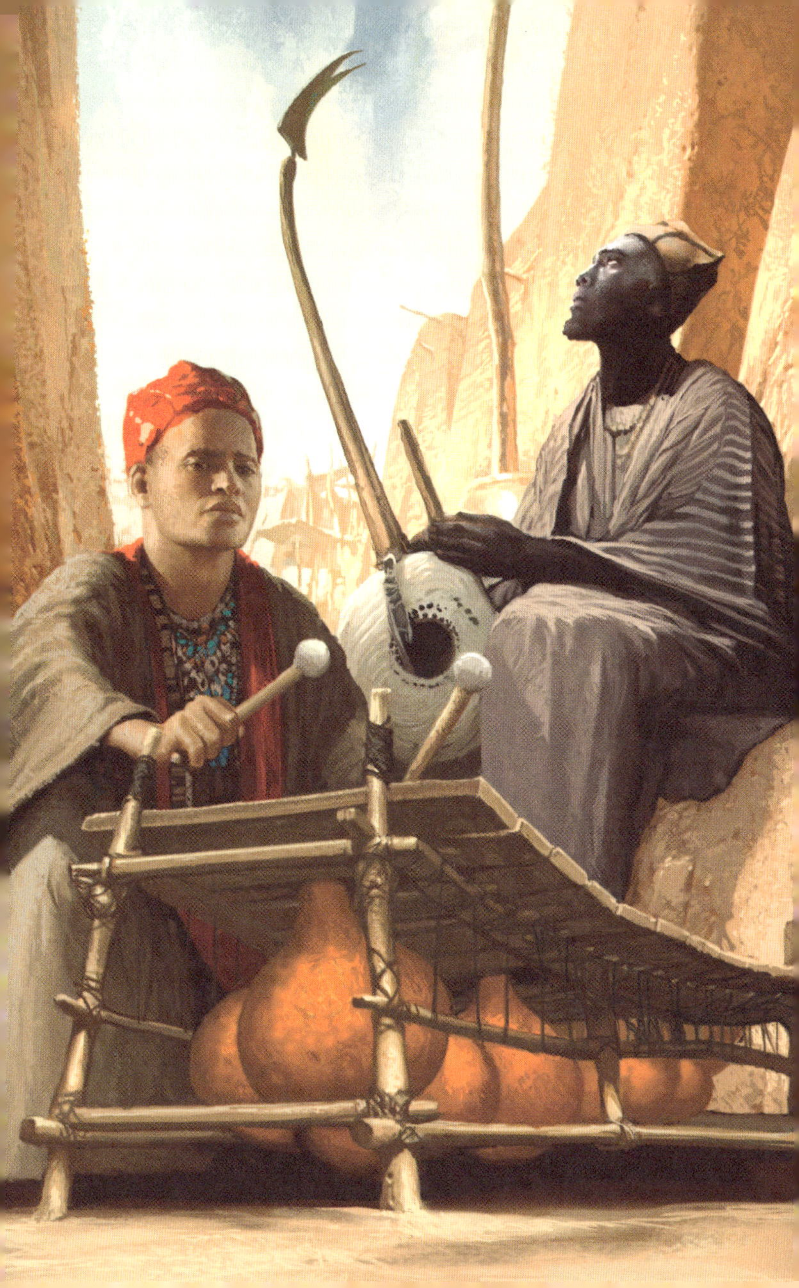

Consolidation of the Empire

After the Battle of Kirina, Emperor Sunjata did not take to the battlefield again. He had attained an almost supernatural status, the living embodiment of the state, of its continuity.

Sunjata left his generals to wage a campaign of near perpetual expansion, extending the Mali Empire westward beyond the bounds of the old Ghana Empire and southwards to the gold-rich forested regions. The empire boasted a standing army of tens of thousands including a large cavalry, who would take to the battlefield armed with lances and swords, and wearing dazzling chain mail and armour. And following on the heels of Sunjata's generals were a legion of administrators and tax collectors, who pulled the newly conquered under the empire's yoke. For a thousand miles, east to west, people bowed to the Mansa.

And as it would be told and retold, the Epic of Sunjata had come to a glorious close – but it was simply the opening chapter of a broader saga, the story of the largest empire West Africa has ever seen.

The Mali Empire became an imperial machine, voraciously devouring its adversaries, and when it ran out of enemies, it conquered its allies and neighbours. Most simply capitulated, yielding to the empire's awe-inspiring and irresistible forces.

It was a state that quickly learned how to work with the demographic complexity of its peoples, allowing its diverse vassal kingdoms and principalities autonomy as long as they paid taxes, showed respect, and were prepared to take to the battlefield when called. Islam became increasingly culturally useful, a universal, binding set of beliefs and a way of life that spread with the growing reach of the empire.

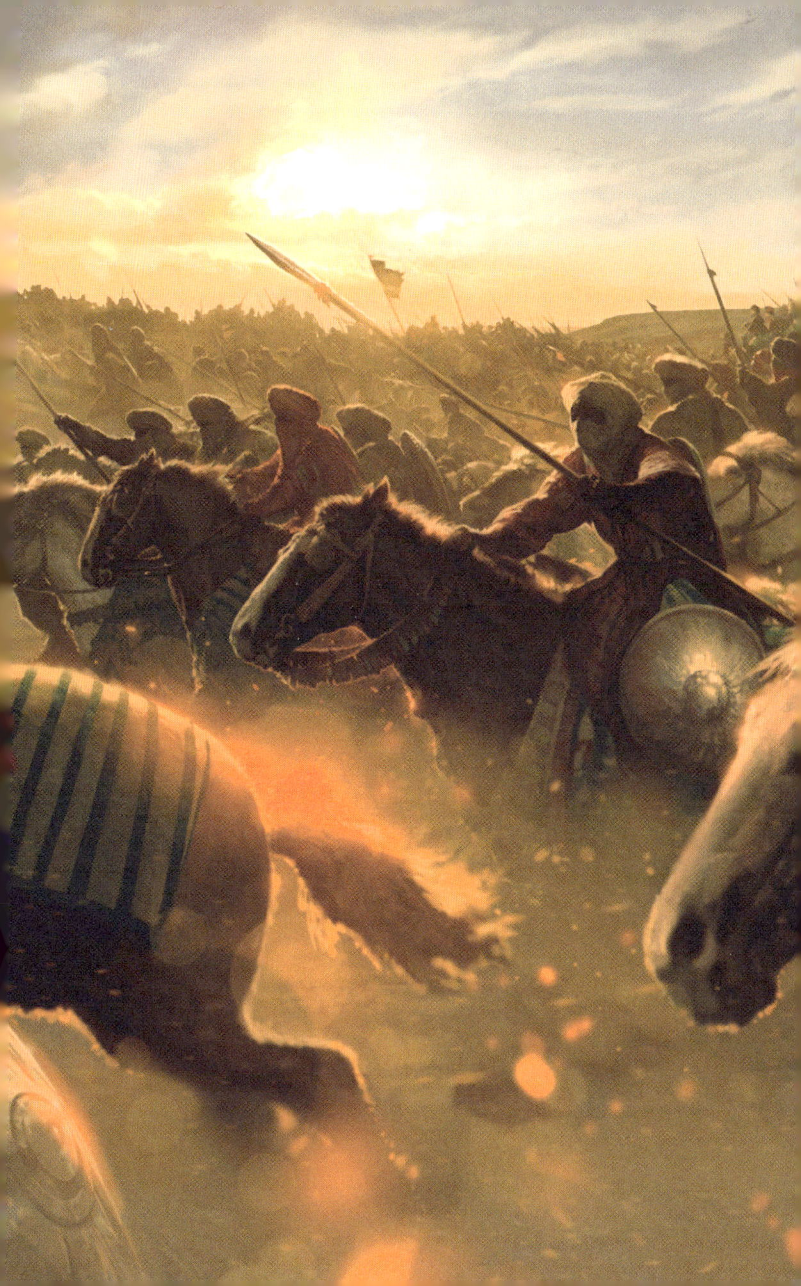

Islam and the Mali Empire

Within the lifetime of Muhammad, Islam had reached Africa. The great cosmopolitan and intellectually tolerant cities of seventh-century North Africa were seen as places of sanctuary for the Prophet's often persecuted followers. Religious scholars and their ideas travelled along the intercontinental trade routes, working across what is today Egypt down into Sudan and Ethiopia, simultaneously traversing the Sahara into West Africa. Islam found a distinct identity in Africa, and many regard Islam as an African religion.

In West Africa, early Islam fitted into a regional context of many belief systems. Many Muslims would still have engaged in some traditional religious practices. There was a widespread acceptance of a liberal form of Malikite Sunnism, in which women did not generally wear veils, and the canonization of celebrated local figures was commonplace. Even today, some dedicated Muslims in this region continue to wear charms and symbols of traditional African religious practice, and will turn to indigenous practices when they are unwell, and builders who construct mosques might utilize pre-Islamic blessings to bring good luck to their congregations.

According to Al-Bakri, the Cordoban writer, Mali rulers converted to Islam before the rise of Sunjata, but they remained tolerant towards traditional religions. When the Berber scholar Ibn Battuta visited the Mali Empire in the fourteenth century, he watched a traditional masquerade with barely disguised disgust, unable to understand why an ostensibly Islamic culture would not just tolerate such practices, but celebrate them at court.

This was a region that thrived on beautiful ideas, and was not prepared to relinquish practices that simply worked.

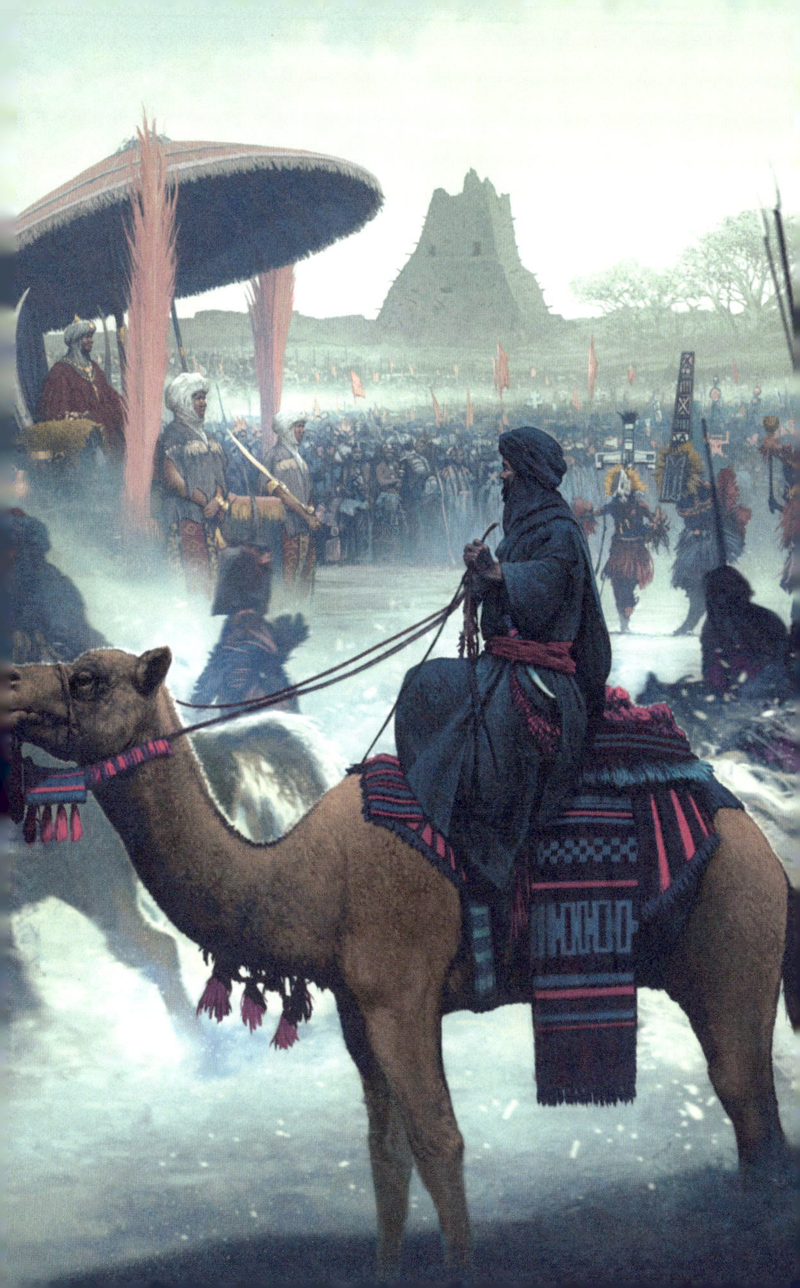

The Desert Trade and the Mali Empire

It was trade that drove and dynamized the region, that kept the great networks across the Sahara open. There were four main routes across the Sahara that would carry goods like salt southward and return with gold. The most important was the two-month camel journey from Sijilmasa, one of the great Maghreb cities, to the West African frontier towns suspended on the edge of the desert, held there by the seasonal generosity of the flooding River Niger. It was towns like Timbuktu – on, or just beyond, the fringes of the empire – that became vital ports for salt-laden caravans travelling southward, and the returning gold that they supplied became critical to the economies of the whole of North Africa, Europe and the Levant. These trading terminuses grew steadily in population and importance.

After Sunjata's death, the stability that he worked so hard to achieve began to evaporate and a succession of his sons fought to hold the empire together. But it was a Spartacus-like figure, Mansa Sakura, a freed slave who had risen to become a general in the imperial army, who used his position to steady the ship, taking control of the failing kingdom to return it to its expansionist tradition. The North African historian and traveller Ibn Khaldun described how Mansa Sakura recaptured the imperial momentum of Sunjata, expanding the empire along the Guinea River to absorb Gao on the edge of the Sahara, to further consolidate Mali's regional dominance. But even as Mansa Sakura sat surveying his now almost complete control of West Africa, he looked spiritually eastward. He was a devout Muslim who felt compelled to make the journey to Mecca – only to be murdered on the journey home by Saharan robbers.

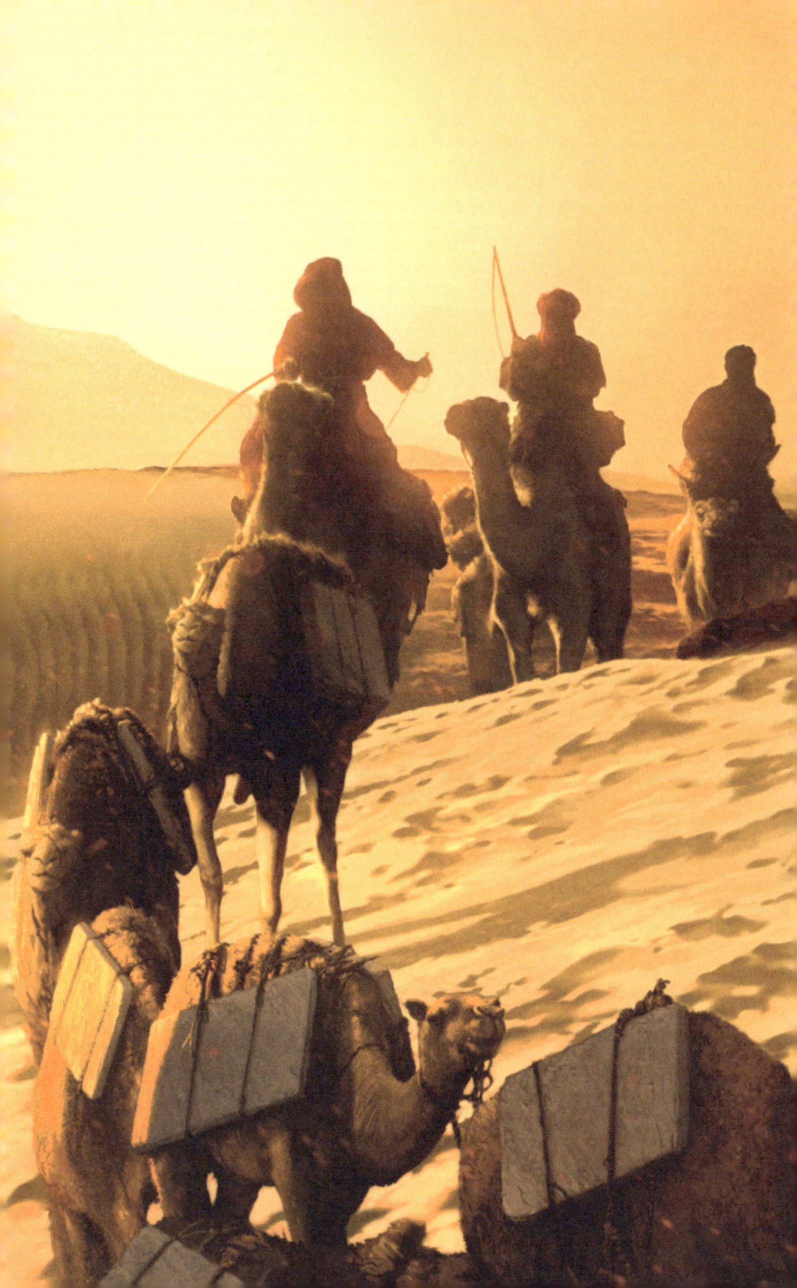

The Voyager King

Abu Bakr, the last direct descendant of Sunjata, ascended the throne at the beginning of the fourteenth century. Abu Bakr Keita, the Voyager King, was as ambitious as his forefathers, but his kingdom was bounded by the Sahara on one side and the Atlantic on the other, leaving him scant options for expansion.

Like the contemporary monarchs of the Portuguese *Reconquista*, or the early Ming dynasty through the achievements of Admiral Zheng He, Abu Bakr Keita would look to his navy to redefine his state, and the sea would become synonymous with his rule.

Mansa Musa, who served as the Abu Bakr's councillor and heir apparent, watched the Emperor's aspiration for expansion grow into an obsession and later recalled how that fixation ultimately led to his downfall. Mansa Musa had witnessed Abu Bakr's sponsorship of a failed attempt to conquer the Atlantic Ocean. The Emperor had bid farewell to hundreds of ships, telling his captains not to return until they had sailed to the far reaches of the Atlantic, and then lamented when only a single vessel returned. Abu Bakr was undeterred. Leaving Mansa Musa to administer his empire in 1312, he tried again. This time, he personally led the expedition, travelling with thousands of fully laden ships.

Neither the Emperor nor his ships were ever seen again, and later that year Mansa Musa ascended the throne.

After years of instability, Mansa Musa was desperate to return to the days of imperial glory, with his whole empire focused around truly fitting objectives – but unlike Sunjata, Mansa Musa had all the power, money and territory he could desire. He would have to find his own frontiers to traverse, to define a new paradigm by which to measure success.

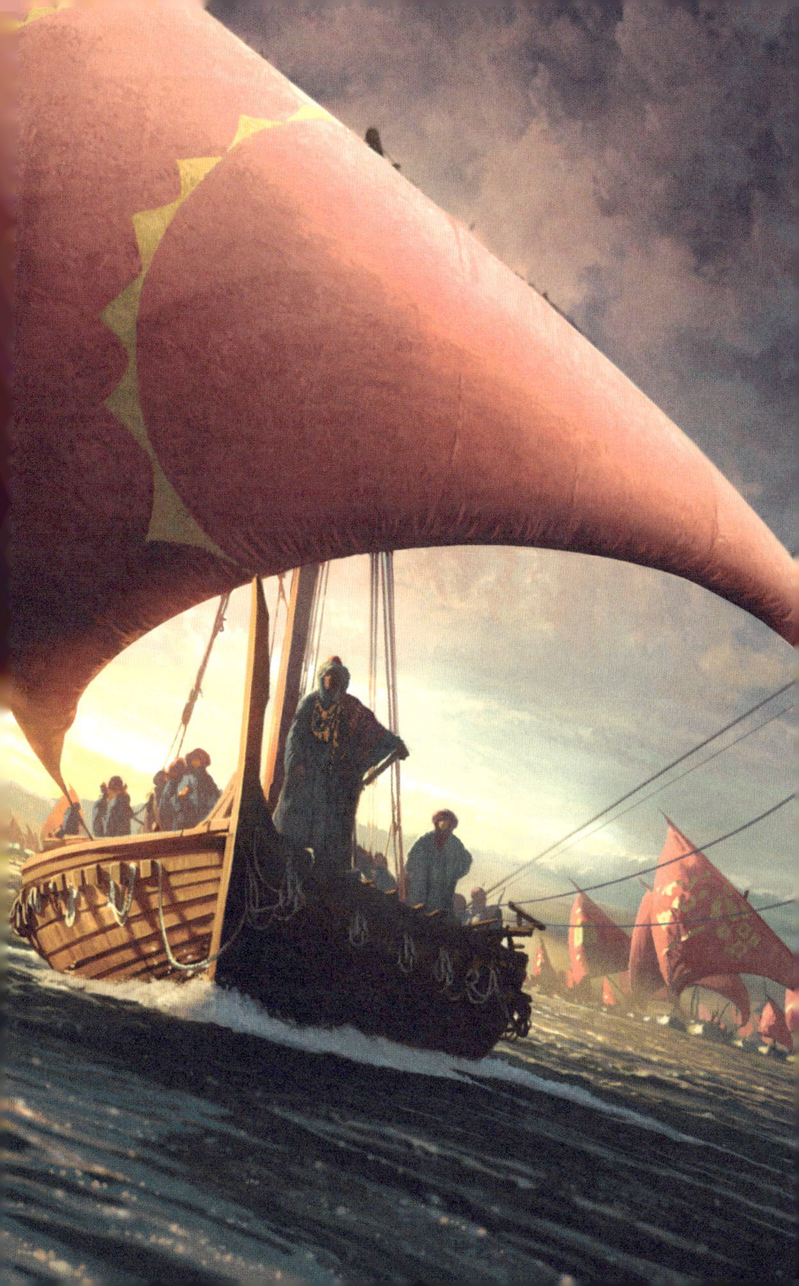

Mansa Musa

Early in his reign Mansa Musa tried to stamp his authority on the empire, and suggest a tonal shift between his reign and those of his predecessors. He was never the playboy prince, and as emperor he wanted Mali to be a more reflective and devout empire.

Unsurprisingly, he faltered in his first steps. When he tried to outlaw traditional religious practices amongst his gold miners, they resisted and output from the mines fell. Mansa Musa capitulated, and gold production returned to its usual output levels. The young Mansa Musa absorbed an important lesson about governance, about how even for an emperor, leadership was built on a certain amount of compromise.

After these early mistakes, Mansa Musa worked to give his subjects and their trading partners what they wanted: security. The Emperor worked with his general, Sagmandia, to secure and police the trade routes, ridding the countryside of bandits and opening up the Mali Empire to an even greater intensity of trans-Saharan trade. Beyond the traditional exchange of salt from the mines of Taghaza in the Western Sahara and gold from the Akan mines to the south, the Sahara opened up to silks from China, spices from India and Persian fabrics. Metalwork came from Europe and Arabian horses – which were predominantly exchanged for gold and copper – grew popular.

But merely to be a better emperor was not enough. Mansa Musa didn't just want wealth and power; he sought knowledge, and he pursued it with the focus and dedication of a general waging a major campaign.

Africa

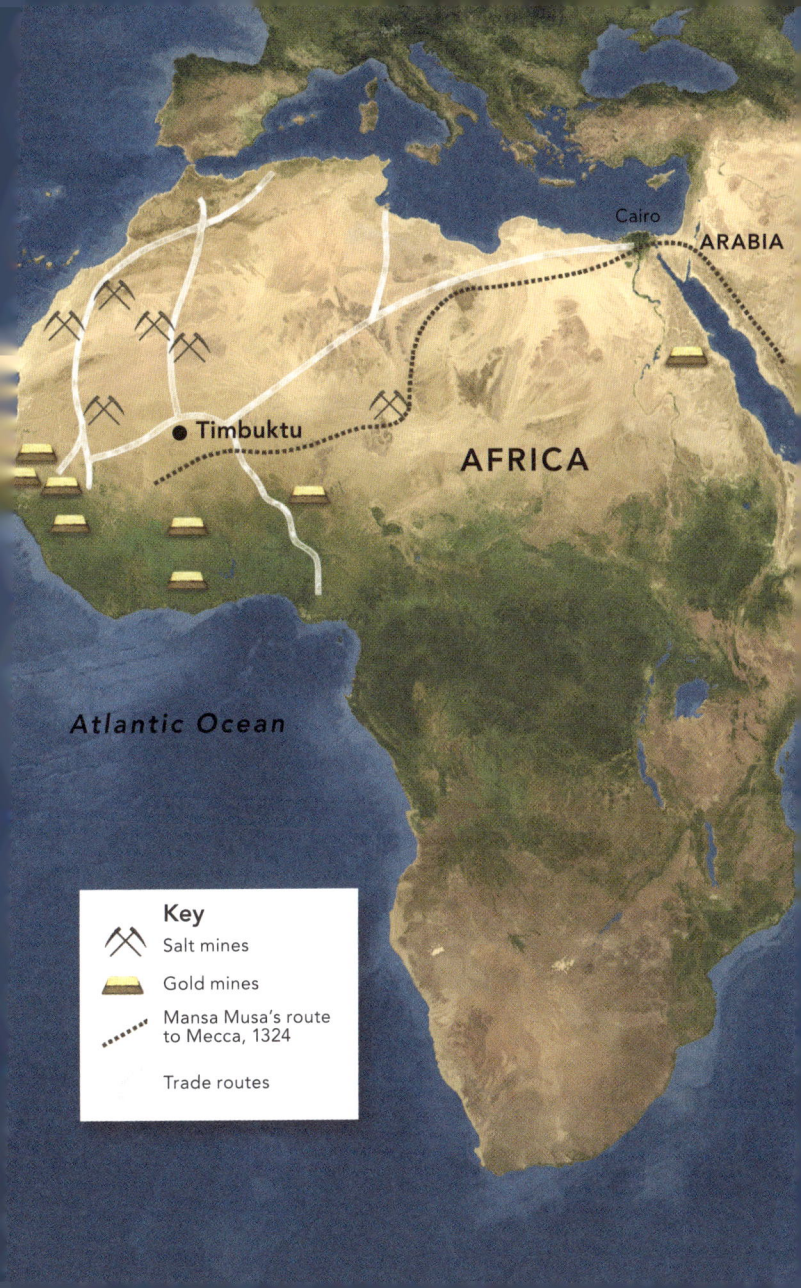

Cairo

ARABIA

Timbuktu

AFRICA

Atlantic Ocean

Key
- Salt mines
- Gold mines
- ········ Mansa Musa's route to Mecca, 1324
- Trade routes

The Great Hajj

The last of the five pillars of Islam is to undertake a pilgrimage, or Hajj. If they have the resources, Muslims are called upon to make the journey to Mecca.

Musa certainly had the resources. The trip from medieval Mali to Mecca was not one that could be undertaken lightly, but a number of earlier emperors had made the journey. The Mansa was an excellent rider and had stables of Arabian horses. Whilst his predecessor might have taken on the 2,000 miles of the Atlantic from West Africa, the journey to Mecca was perhaps as difficult. It was at least three times further, and across some of the most unforgiving terrain on Earth.

In 1324, twelve or so years after becoming emperor, 60,000 people left the Mali Empire with Mansa Musa. Most would walk every hard mile to Mecca. Some years later, the Arab scholar Shihab Al-Umari described this extraordinary retinue as being made up of 8,000 soldiers, 12,000 personal staff, members of the Emperor's court and ordinary citizens, followed by eighty camels, each bearing 300 lbs of gold. Each night when they stopped, it was said to be like a whole town decamping in the desert. And they took with them everything they needed, including a mosque, which they would construct so that the Emperor could pray. The logistical complexity of shepherding so many people across an arid landscape safely would have been every bit as testing as waging a military campaign, or navigating a fleet across the Atlantic.

No one had ever engaged upon the journey to Mecca in such style.

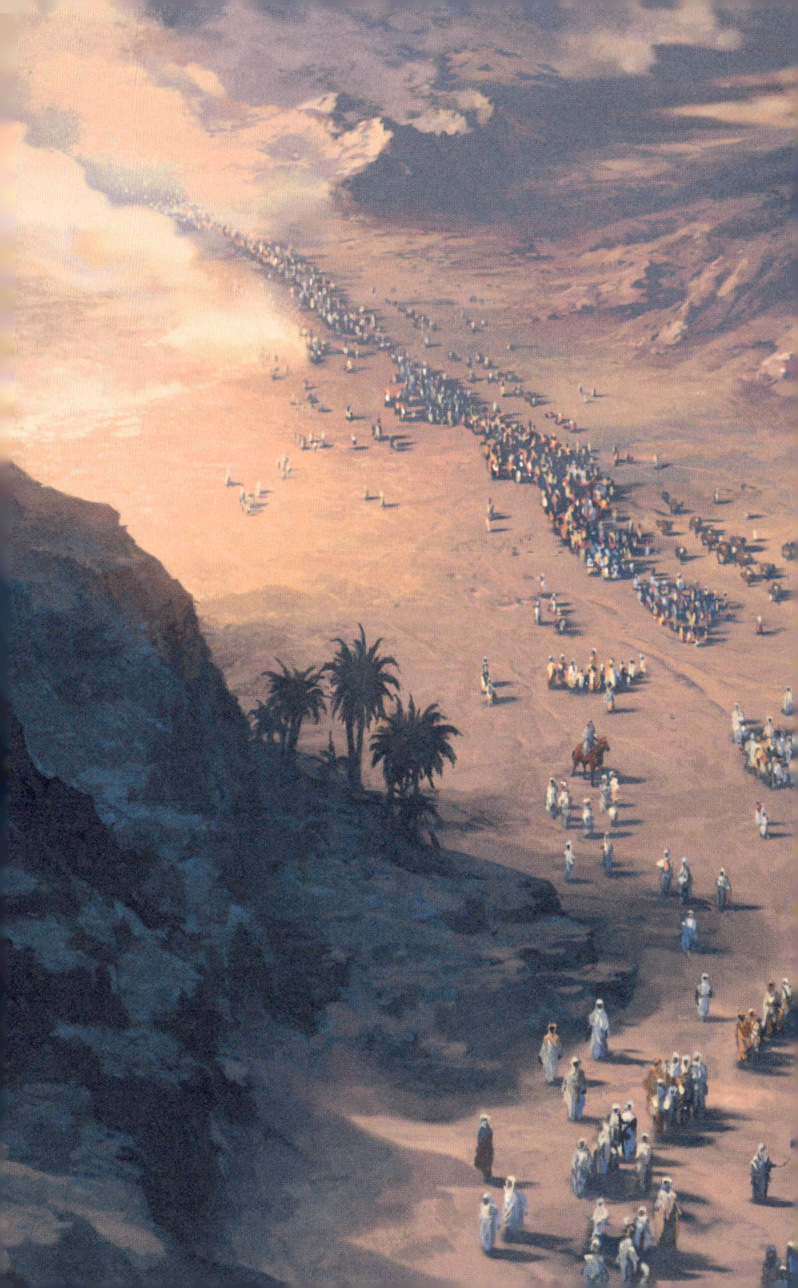

Cairo

Mansa Musa's arrival in Cairo in July 1324 was greeted with celebrations. Al-Maqrizi, the Egyptian historian, captured Mansa Musa's arrival: 'He is a young man with brown skin, a pleasant face and good figure, instructed in Malikite rite. He appeared amidst his companions magnificently dressed and mounted, and surrounded by more than 10,000 subjects. He brought gifts and presents that amazed the eye with their beauty and splendour.' The Mamluk Sultan, Al-Nasir Muhammad, perhaps recognizing Mansa Musa as the richest man who had ever lived, ordered his city to give the visiting emperor a fitting welcome.

Yet even Mansa Musa was, according to Egyptian etiquette, meant to bow to his host, the Sultan. But rather than show his subservience to the Sultan as was customary, Mansa Musa kissed the ground in praise of Allah and was welcomed to court. Mansa Musa was a natural diplomat, he knew he must accept local mores, but he was not about to bow to anyone. The Sultan was won over, inviting Mansa Musa to shelter in Cairo over the summer, perhaps knowing that this hugely wealthy man might bring benefit to the city's economy with his generosity. It has been often repeated, that Mansa Musa spent and gave away so much gold that the economic repercussions of his visit were felt for a decade.

When the cooler weather arrived, Mansa Musa and his caravan pushed on to Mecca.

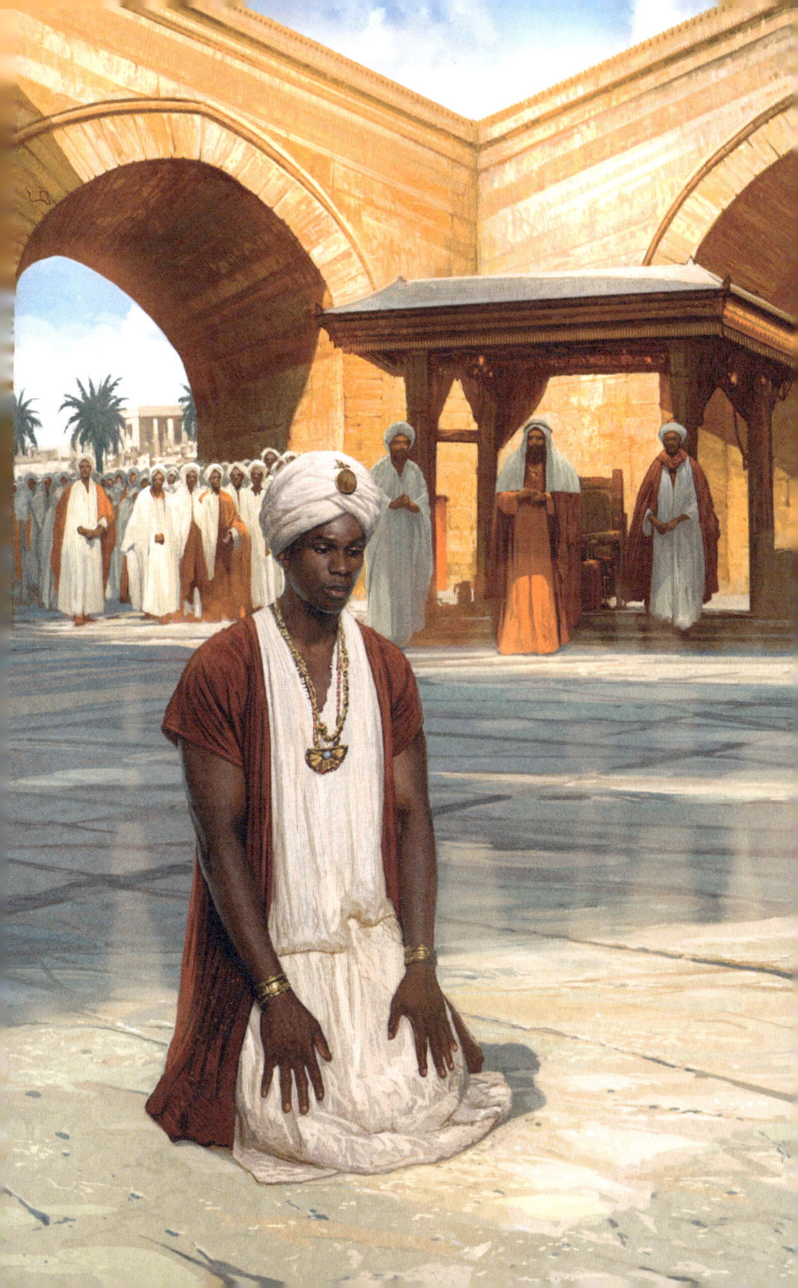

Mecca

For the days that Mansa Musa spent at Mecca, he would have worn no finery, dressing like any other pilgrim, praying as, and with, the other worshippers.

After completing his pilgrimage, he stayed to meet some of the great Islamic scholars and imams. Over the period of Hajj, areas of Mecca attracted some of the finest thinkers of the age. One can imagine that he may well have met scholars who had travelled from the newly established university at Salamanca, from the ancient Berber centres of intellectual excellence like Al-Qarawiyyin, or perhaps scholars who had followed him on the last leg from Cairo's Al-Azhar Mosque. Some would have doubtless hailed from the courts of Venice, or the madrassas of the burgeoning Ottoman Empire, and we know that Mansa Musa was left utterly entranced. As he made arrangements to return, he invited a number of these intellectuals and a group who claimed to be descendants of the Prophet, to return to Niani with him. Amongst them was one of the greatest poets and architects of the age, Abu Ishaq Al-Sahili, who had learned his trade under the formidable Berber architects of Granada.

As much as being a pilgrimage, it was also a statement to the world about the wealth, ambition and intellectual culture of Mali. The news of his journey created waves that would reverberate across the Middle-East and Europe. Fifty years later, Abraham Cresques, the cartographer, would immortalize Mansa Musa, holding a gold nugget, at the centre of the great Catalan Atlas made for Charles V. It is an image of a particular kind of African wisdom and wealth that would become a point of inspiration for European artists for centuries to come.

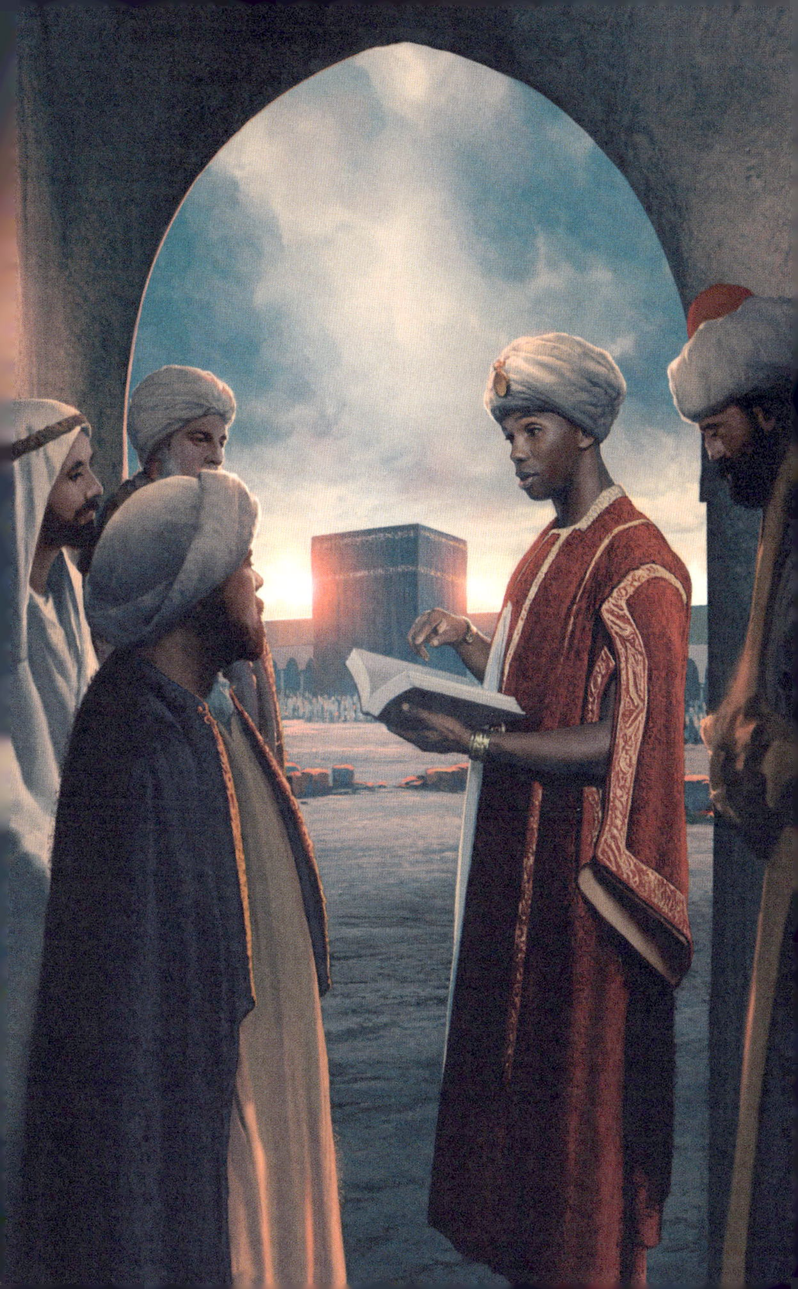

Journey Home

Mansa Musa must have known that his predecessor, Mansa Sakura, had completed the Hajj, only to be murdered in the desert on the return journey. If he was to write his place into history, he would have to craft his homeward journey with as much care as he had his Hajj. But Mansa Musa had spent so much gold, had been so generous, that on his way back through Cairo he had to take out loans (possibly some of the very gold that he had previously given away), to make sure that the return leg across the Sahara was undertaken with the necessary style and safety.

With his caravan replenished, he re-entered the desert. And, perhaps to reassert his invulnerability, when his second wife complained of feeling dusty, his engineers were apparently ordered to construct a complex irrigation system to channel water over dozens of metres, through oiled channels, to fill her bath.

Like the Berber dynasties who demonstrated their might and sophistication through extravagant water engineering, Mansa Musa wanted to be remembered. He was the greatest Mali emperor and the wealthiest man on Earth, he presided over the largest empire West Africa had ever seen, and he wanted his people – and now the whole world – never to forget what that meant. Neither the most formidable desert on Earth nor the most extravagant Hajj in history would be a challenge to him.

In 1325, he returned a changed man, who wanted to bring some of what he had seen in Mecca home with him. Not just to return with books and intellectuals, but to institute new traditions and attitudes towards learning. His empire would not sit on the world's periphery; it would be the centre of a new world.

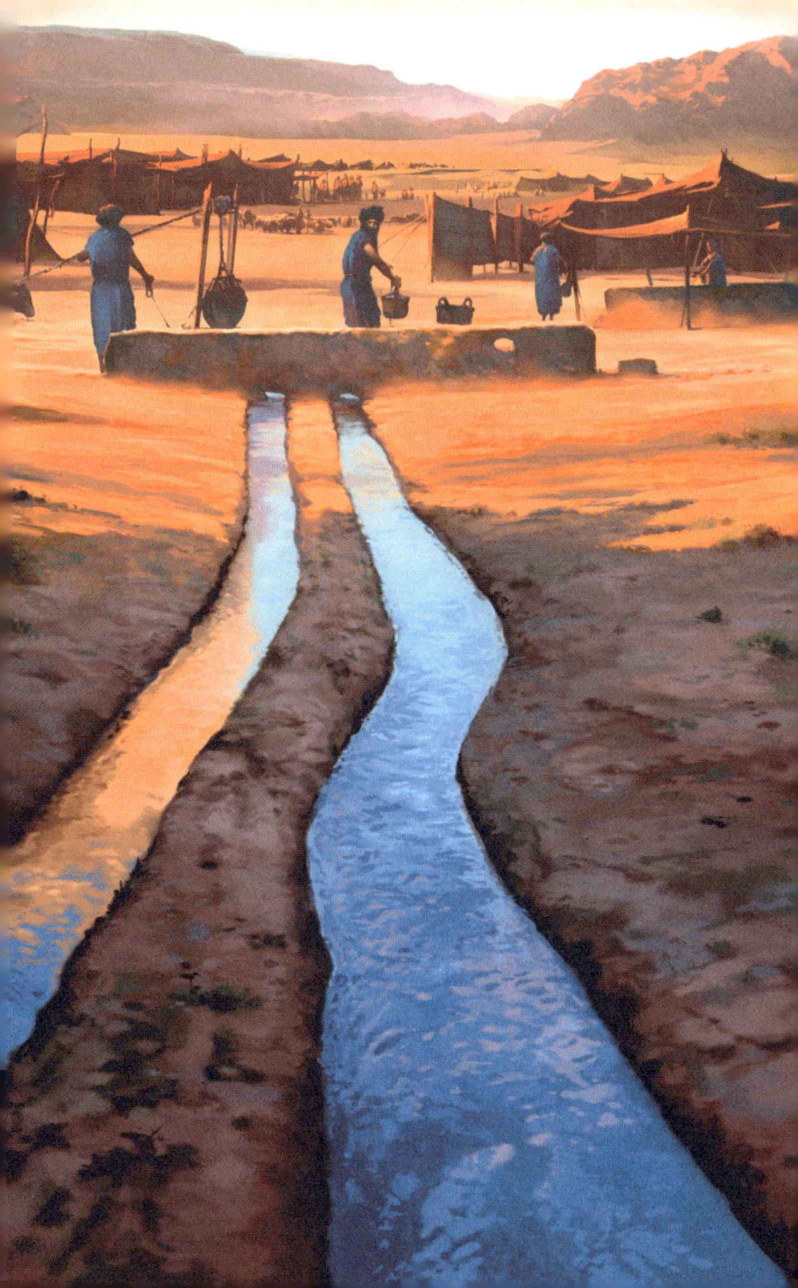

Timbuktu

Whilst still some distance from home, Mansa Musa received a missive from his general Sagmandia that his forces had recaptured Gao for the empire. Overjoyed by the news of the reconquering of this frontier of his empire, Mansa Musa decided to delay his immediate return to Niani and to visit Gao instead, to receive the public submission of the Songhai king. To win over this wayward city on the outer edge of his empire, he spent time with the King, commissioning his architect to build a new mosque and taking two of the King's sons with him to join his court.

They travelled on via another reconquered Songhai town, Timbuktu. And there, on the edge of the desert, Mansa Musa fell in love.

The city was more than just a trading port for nomadic pastoralists. It had grown up around the old Sankore Mosque, established in 989 by the magistrate of Timbuktu, Al-Qadi Aqib ibn Mahmud ibn Umar. The inner courtyard of the old mosque shared the exact dimensions of the Ka'bah, the shrine that sits in the quad of the Great Mosque at Mecca. Timbuktu was already a great centre of intellectual excellence, with a significant student body. The atmosphere in Timbuktu must have been reminiscent of the gatherings of intellectuals that transfixed Mansa Musa at Mecca – polishing this jewel on the most easterly tip of his empire would be his great legacy. Even though it was a thousand miles from his capital in Niani, and many months' travel from his empire's western border, Timbuktu would be Mansa Musa's Florence. It would be the place where he would invest his love – as close to Mecca as his kingdom allowed. Here, in this multi-ethnic city of Songhai, Arabic and Tamashagh cultures, he would deposit his extensive collection of valuable documents.

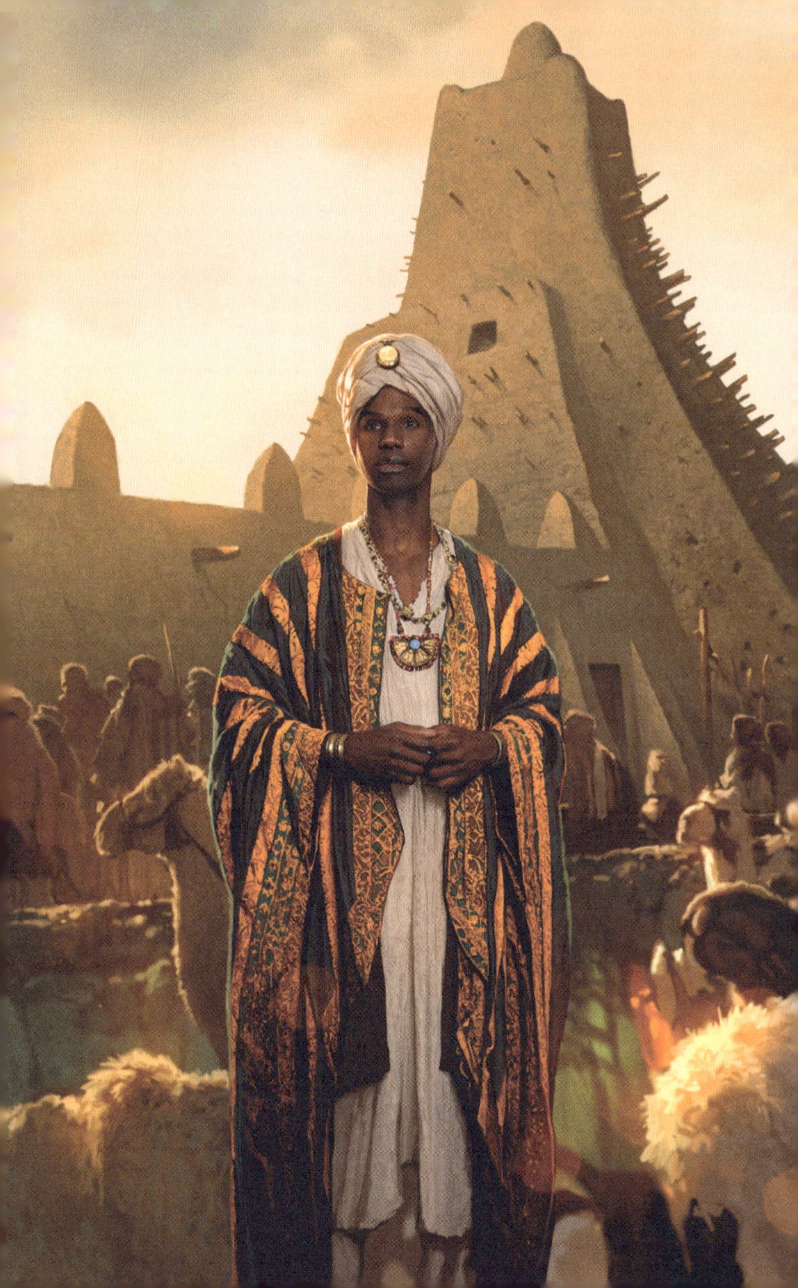

The Renewed Timbuktu

Mansa Musa engaged his seer-like architect, Abu Ishaq Al-Sahili, to construct a spectacular madugu or palace and a great mosque for his new Timbuktu. According to the Berber historian Ibn Khaldun, the builder was paid 12,000 mithkals in gold (the equivalent of more than £1.5 million) – and in return Al-Sahili gave Timbuktu the Djingereyber Mosque, one of the finest buildings ever created. The complex of buildings was constructed from the materials that are still utilized in the region today: wet earth mixed with straw, moulded and fashioned around a timber structure to create well-insulated buildings that are organically shaped and strong enough to withstand the ferocious desert winds and occasional rains. When it was complete, the Djingereyber Mosque comprised inner courtyards and prayer space for a congregation of 2,000. It was an architectural masterpiece, and remains one of the most iconic buildings in Africa.

Over the next decade, the Sankore and the Djingereyber mosques, and the buildings around and between them, developed into the most comprehensive and important African archive since the Library of Alexandria. At its peak, Timbuktu could accommodate 25,000 students, and housed at least 400,000 – perhaps as many as 800,000 – manuscripts. The city was a match for the most respected universities in Europe. And around these key madrassas grew up a community of private libraries, publishers and booksellers, some of whom became hugely wealthy.

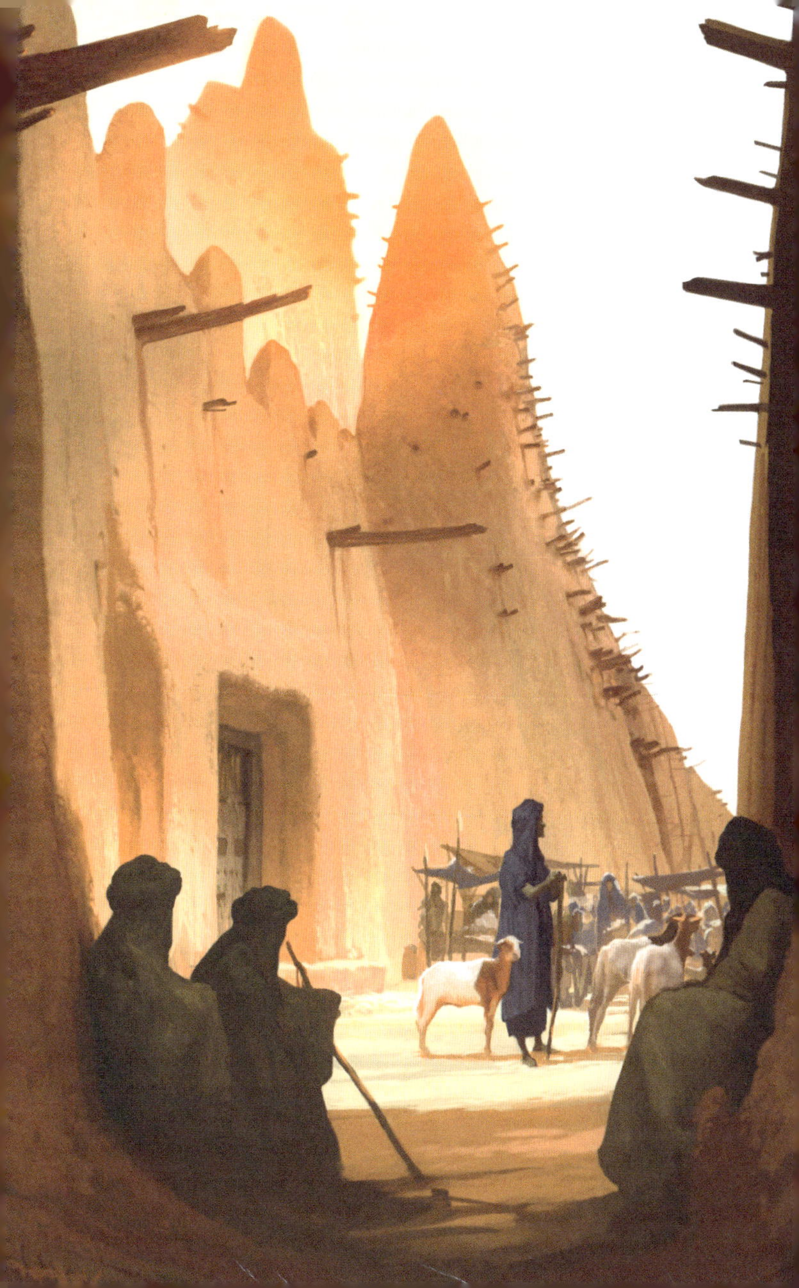

Sankore

In some ways Sankore was not like a European university. It had no central senate, but was made up of independent madrassas and libraries, each led by its own imam or scholar. Yet there were also many ways that it did resemble a medieval European university – students met in the courtyards, rooms and corridors of mosques and houses to learn about subjects like Arabic, law, history, astronomy, chemistry, philosophy, medicine – and a range of practical trades. At the heart of the curriculum, developed by intellectual luminaries like the Fula jurist Modibo Mohammad Al-Kaburi, were Qur'anic, Islamic and Arabic studies. If we were to transpose Latin for Arabic, and substitute the Qur'an for the Bible, we might be describing a medieval European university.

Like its emperor, the city was driven by a pursuit of innovative and rigorous thinking. Even whilst acknowledging the underpinning of formal religion, the Mali Empire was a culturally liberal state which accommodated the finest academic ideas and invention from wherever they came. Within this city's confines, some of the most radical medieval thinking would take root: invention in areas as varied as mathematics and human rights. The highest academic degree could take a decade to complete, and as Timbuktu's prestige and reputation grew, it drew students and academics from across West and North Africa, from the great madrassas of Mecca, Fez, Tunis and Cairo.

Whilst Timbuktu might have been established on Mali's easterly border, looking outward across the desert, it quickly became a confident, intellectually distinctive centre which had its own powerful gravitational pull.

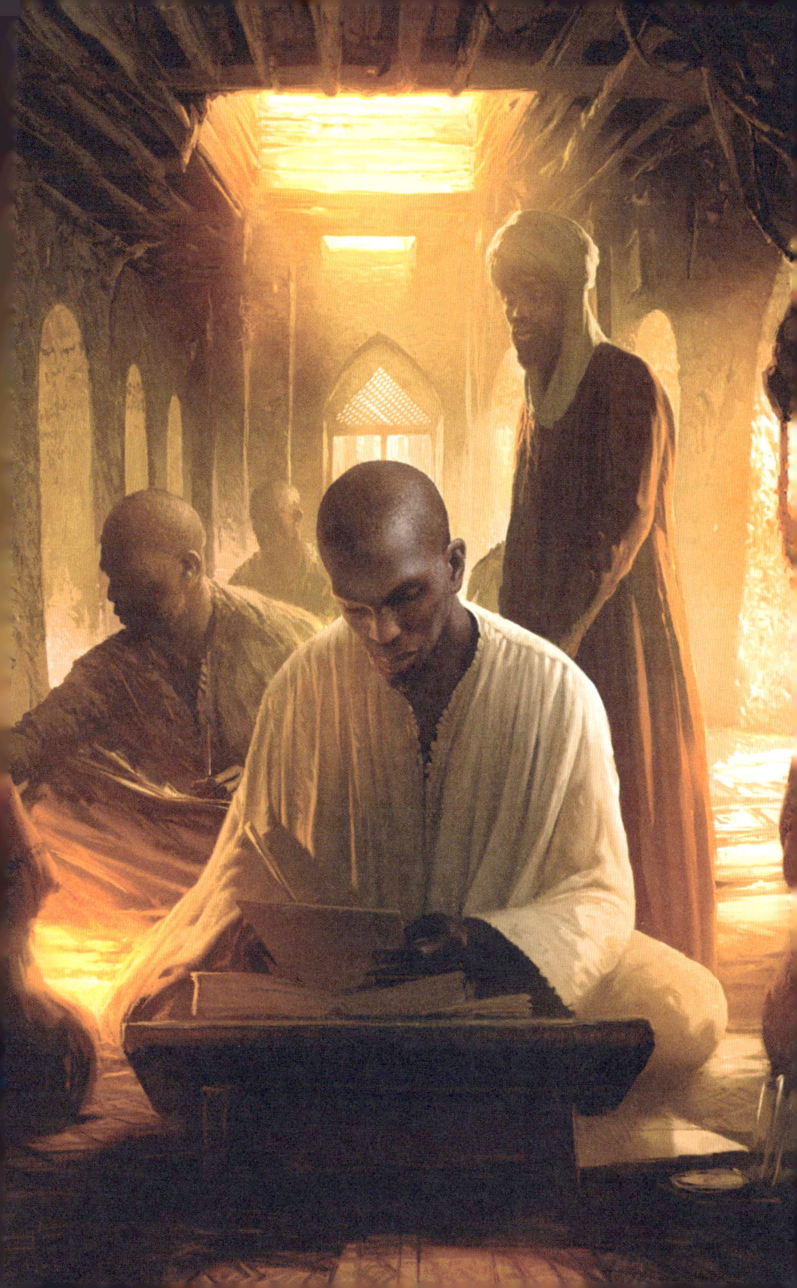

The Libraries

The collection of books held in the sixty-plus Timbuktu archives offer a fascinating glimpse into the medieval African perspective on the wider world. They give us vivid access to an intellectually voracious and innovative state which drew in the most cutting-edge thinking from all over the region and beyond.

Amongst many hundreds of thousands of texts are documents presented in the form of a Platonic discourse outlining Greco-Roman astronomy, appended with developments and discoveries made by Muslim scholars. The libraries include compilations of medical cures, describing methods of diagnosing and treating the sick which include prayers and Qur'anic verses that might be helpful against illness. There are documents setting out the ideal ethical conduct of business and government, including discourses on slavery, which postulate that the fundamental and original state of humanity is autonomous and free.

It is a body of thinking that shows Timbuktu to have been a cosmopolitan city which used the tenets of Islam as a base upon which to configure a state that worked for its citizens and made sense of the world. It represents that rare thing in Africa: material evidence of the continent's unique intellectual innovation and its inter-regional co-development of new ideas. This was a confident state that did not feel itself to be on the world's periphery, but a critical and integrated part of a nexus of cultures that were embracing a moment of burgeoning change, when almost anything seemed possible.

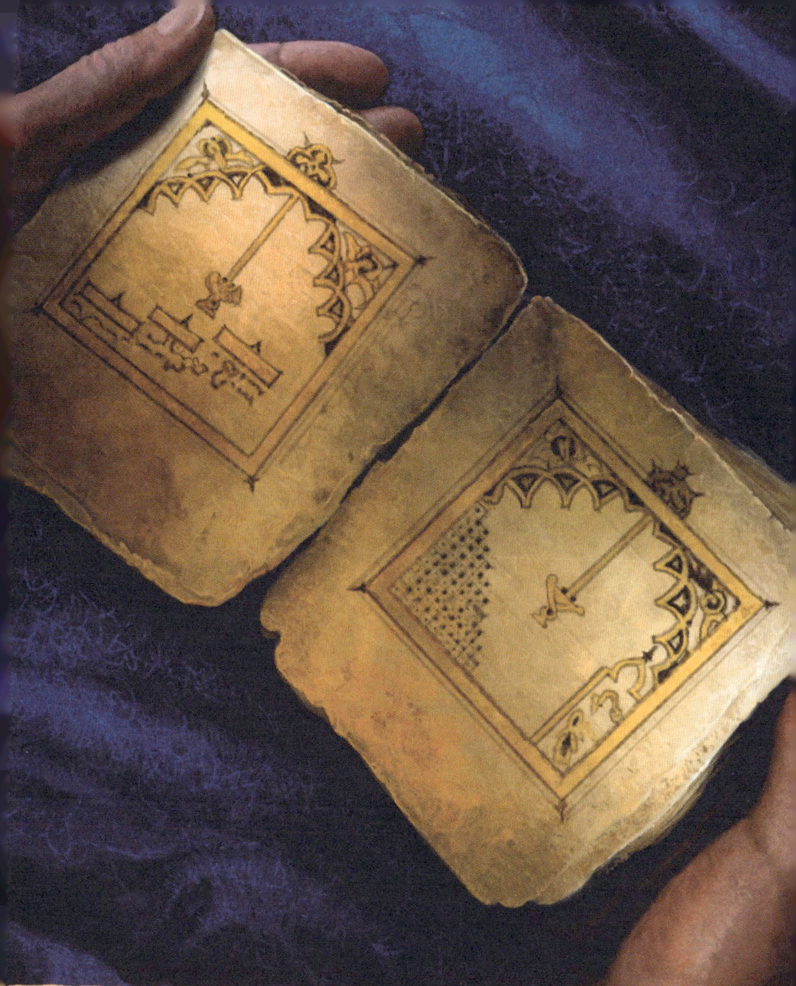

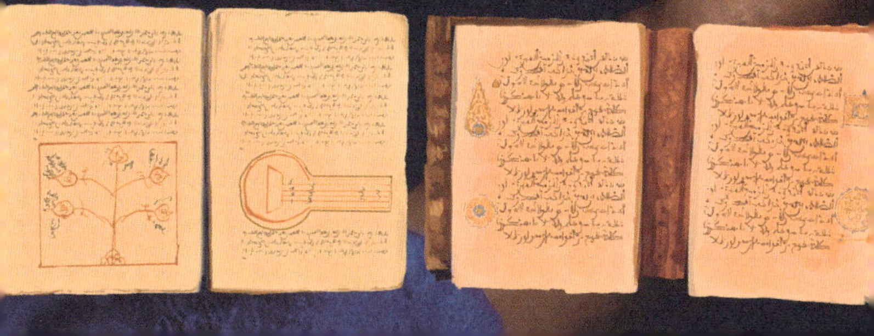

An Empire at its Peak

Mansa Musa's reign was a high-water mark for the Mali Empire: territorially vast and politically relatively stable. Unlike the Ghana Empire, Mali had been able to defend its borders, maintain gold production, feed its population and govern. When Mansa Musa died, he left behind an empire that encompassed what is today Senegal, southern Mauritania, Mali, northern Burkina Faso, western Niger, The Gambia, Guinea-Bissau, Guinea, the Ivory Coast and northern Ghana. And beyond the empire, in its trade and through reputation, it had touched much of the Middle East and the southern Mediterranean.

But perhaps Mansa Musa's greatest legacy was to change the paradigm of the state. Where his Ghana Empire forefathers had invested in systems of oral history, in griots and storytellers, Mansa Musa had fundamentally shifted the culture of record. In consciously supporting writing the history down, he had created a distinction between himself, the emperor's court, and the law. With written record, history, contracts and legislation were no longer fluid things that were arbitrated by the old and powerful. The law had become a set of discrete rules that could not only be corroborated in precedent, but also accessed and utilized by a wider pool of the population. This shift afforded Mali's subjects a greater sense of individual security and redress than West Africans had previously known.

Ironically for the man whose greatest legacy was 'history', we are not sure when Mansa Musa died. We do know that he lived to see his palace and mosque in Timbuktu thriving. Whatever the exact date, with his death also passed a way of life – the golden period of the empire was over.

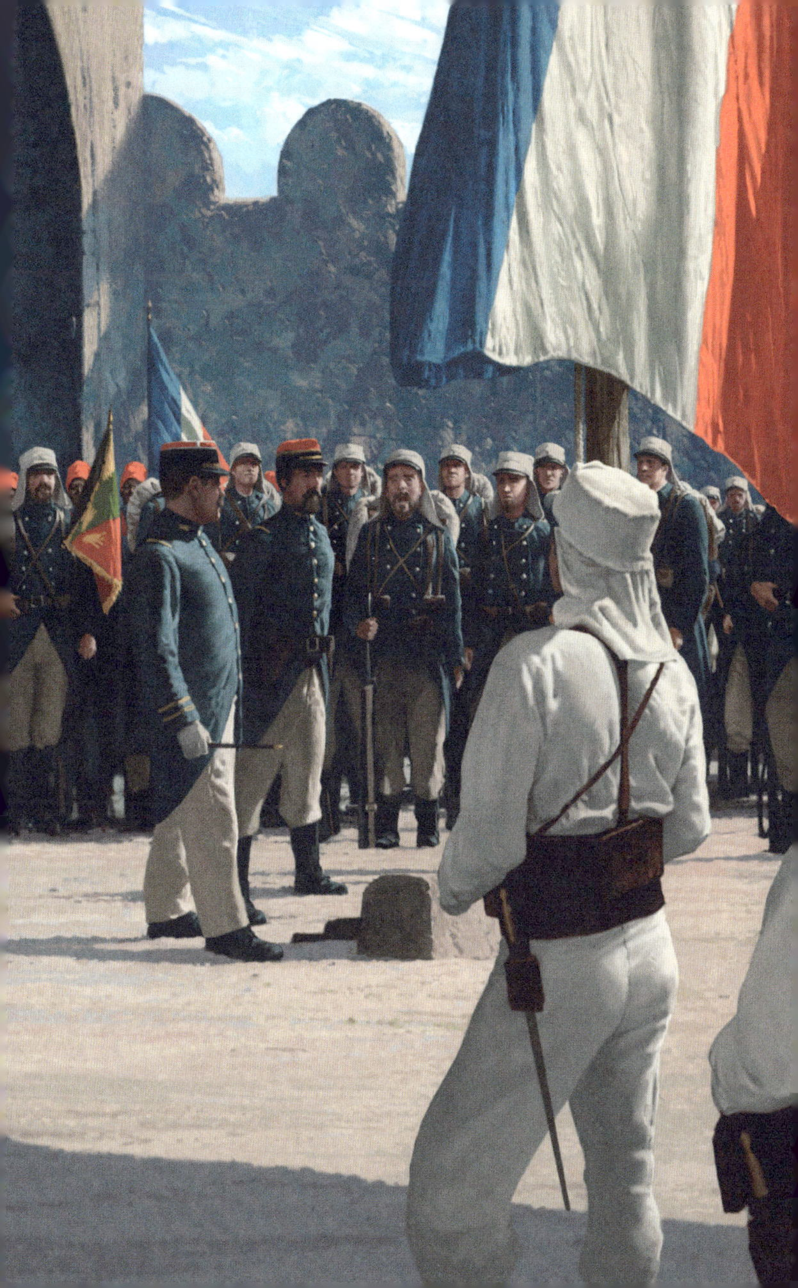

Faltering and Decline

In the years following Mansa Musa's death, history seemed to repeat itself. Just as at the end of Sunjata's reign, the empire began to fray at its extremities. Over decades a catastrophic cascade of territorial losses sent the administration into retreat.

Possibly recognizing the empire's weakened state, the Songhai found renewed confidence, and rose up to make a case for their self-determination. In 1433, the Mali Empire was forced to relinquish its sovereignty of Gao and Timbuktu. The somewhat decrepit empire found itself cut out of a large proportion of the desert trade, and, with its institutions imploding, was forced to yield up territory and political influence to the Songhai.

Under the Songhai, Timbuktu continued to thrive. Over generations, through changes in regional leadership, through military assaults and drought, the city and libraries carried on expanding. This period of development offers an insight not just into the breadth of African intellectual invention, but also into the way that ideas from across the medieval world were exchanged and combined. The desert port on the edge of the Sahara had become increasingly important because of the knowledge and expertise that it uniquely safeguarded, those values of intellectual inquisitiveness and rigour that Mansa Musa had instituted.

When the Berbers invaded the region in 1594, breaking the stronghold of the Songhai and taking Ahmad Baba Al-Timbukti, the most respected academic of the city, into custody, they were aware that knowledge had become this city's great asset – and this would be a pattern that would sadly be replicated in successive invasions.

Colonial Period

Since the early fifteenth century, French merchants and explorers had been building trading relationships with cultures on the West African coast. In 1659, they established a permanent presence, constructing a collection of fortified buildings from which to manage their trade on the island of Saint Louis off the coast of what is today Senegal. Over the next 300 years, French territories were to grow to encompass vast areas of West Africa. With the great rationalization of European colonial power in West Africa in the late nineteenth century, various French colonial territories were consolidated into a region that resembled what had once constituted the Mali Empire.

The peoples of these vast territories were subject to French law, but they were not citizens. Their French education system taught them about rights which they were not able to exercise, and the republic's founding principles of liberty, equality and fraternity were starkly absent. It was a situation that could not be endured for long. The highly educated West African population fell upon their age-old tradition of book learning and education to fight back, training generations of lawyers to advocate against colonial encroachments. And with the fall of the Vichy Government in 1942, emboldened French West Africans began to petition for citizenship rights, and to fight for greater autonomy and then independence. After the Second World War, France attempted to reimagine its relationship with its colonies by establishing a French union, affording West Africans many of the rights they had previously been denied, but it was too little, too late. With the collapse of French control in Indo-China and then North Africa, the colonial moment had passed.

Enduring Tradition

When Ansa Dine, an Al-Qaeda-affiliated militia, attacked Timbuktu in 2012, claiming that they wanted to purge the city of idolatrous documents, irreligious buildings and shrines, ordinary Malians risked their safety to protect the city and its heritage.

Ansa Dine's campaign wasn't simply vandalism. The attempted destruction of nine tombs, the central mosque and perhaps as many as 4,000 manuscripts was a considered act. The underlying aim was to destroy the stories that connected people to the age of Sunjata, and in so doing, to destroy the Mali Empire narrative. They even attempted to suppress the playing of the kora and balofon (the instruments legendarily adopted on the battlefield when the Mali Empire was founded). Like Mansa Musa, they understood the power of narrative to hold communities together, and by contrast hoped that in destroying stories, they might destroy a people.

Thankfully, this was a history that still resonated with its cultural heirs. Over the long, difficult months of 2012, the local population worked to secrete and smuggle documents to safety, doing what they could to protect historic buildings and defend Timbuktu's libraries. Although they were not always successful, many of the manuscripts were thankfully saved, and by 2015 each of the shrines damaged during the uprising was rebuilt, and Mansa Musa's mosque, the symbolic heart of the city, was restored. Although the struggle remains far from over, the city continues to reaffirm its connection to its past and to publicly and proudly safeguard an open and tolerant way of life.